NBA CHAMPIONSHIP:

1971

ALL-TIME LEADING SCORER:

KAREEM ABDUL-JABBAR (1969–75):

14,211 POINTS

BUCKS
12

THE NBA: A HISTORY OF HOOPS

MILWAUKEE BUCKS

BY JIM WHITING

CREATIVE EDUCATION CREATIVE PAPERBACKS

Published by Creative Education
and Creative Paperbacks

P.O. Box 227, Mankato, Minnesota 56002

Creative Education and Creative Paperbacks
are imprints of The Creative Company

www.thecreativecompany.us

Design and production by Blue Design

Printed in the United States of America

Photographs by AP Images (ASSOCIATED PRESS), Corbis (Matt Brown/NewSport, Steve Lipofsky, JOE SKIPPER/Reuters, FRED THORNHILL/Reuters), Getty Images (Allsport USA/Allsport/Getty Images Sport, Brian Babineau/NBAE, Vernon Biever/NBAE, Kevin C. Cox/Getty Images Sport, Jonathan Daniel/Allsport, Gary Dineen/NBAE, Focus on Sport, Wesley Hitt/Getty Images Sport, Mike McGinnis/Getty Images Sport, Ronald C. Modra/Sports Imagery, Panoramic Images, Dick Raphael/NBAE, David Sherman/NBAE, Damian Strohmeyer/Sports Illustrated), Newscom (Harry E. Walker/MCT)

Library of Congress Cataloging-in-Publication Data

Names: Whiting, Jim, 1943- author.

Title: Milwaukee Bucks / Jim Whiting.

Series: The NBA: A History of Hoops.

Includes bibliographical references and index.

Summary: This high-interest title summarizes the history of the Milwaukee Bucks professional basketball team, highlighting memorable events and noteworthy players such as Ray Allen.

Identifiers: LCCN 2017005588 / ISBN 978-1-60818-851-2 (hardcover) / ISBN 978-1-62832-454-9 (pbk) / ISBN 978-1-56660-899-2 (eBook)

Subjects: LCSH: 1. Milwaukee Bucks (Basketball team)—History—Juvenile literature. 2. Milwaukee Bucks (Basketball team)—Biography—Juvenile literature.

Classification: LCC GV885.52.M54 W47 2017 / DDC 796.323/640977595—dc23

CCSS: RI.4.1, 2, 3, 4; RI.5.1, 2, 4; RI.6.1, 2, 3; RF.4.3, 4; RF.5.3, 4; RH. 6-8. 4, 5, 7

First Edition HC 9 8 7 6 5 4 3 2 1

First Edition PBK 9 8 7 6 5 4 3 2 1

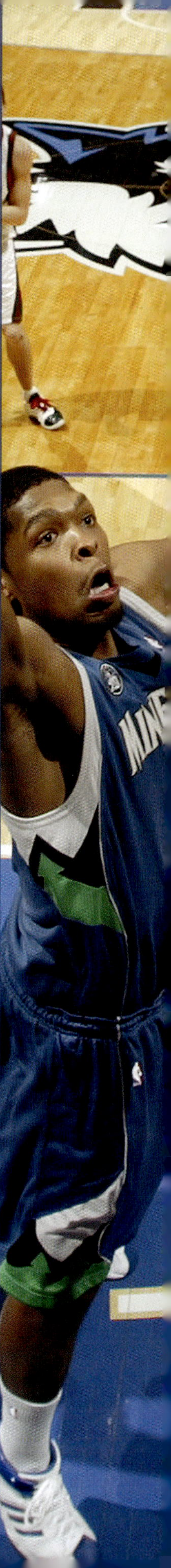

BUCKS
22
MINNESOTA
3

BUCKS
8
7

CONTENTS

Located on the western shore of Lake Michigan, **MILWAUKEE** is Wisconsin's largest city.

THE BUCKS BEGIN

The Milwaukee Bucks needed to win Game 6 of the 2001 National Basketball Association (NBA) Eastern Conference finals. They trailed the Philadelphia 76ers, 2–3. Playing before nearly 20,000

Known for his flawless form, **RAY ALLEN** sank 1,051 three-pointers with the Bucks.

frenzied fans, the Bucks roared to a 33-point lead. Shooting guard Ray Allen was the key. He had scored 19 points in just 6 minutes. But the 76ers didn't fold. Late in the third quarter, they cut the deficit to 11 points. More than six minutes remained. "We've been known to blow leads," Allen said. "We just had to keep our composure." He did. He sank two quick three-pointers to end the threat. Milwaukee won, 110–100. The series was now tied! Allen had scored 41 points. Twenty-seven of those were three-point shots. That tied the all-time NBA playoff record. The Bucks were confident going into Game 7.

Milwaukee was one of two NBA expansion teams that began playing in the 1968–69 season. When Milwaukee received its franchise, it needed a name. Like many NBA teams, Milwaukee wanted to involve fans in the process. Thousands of people

BUCKS
34
SIXERS
40
SIXERS
20

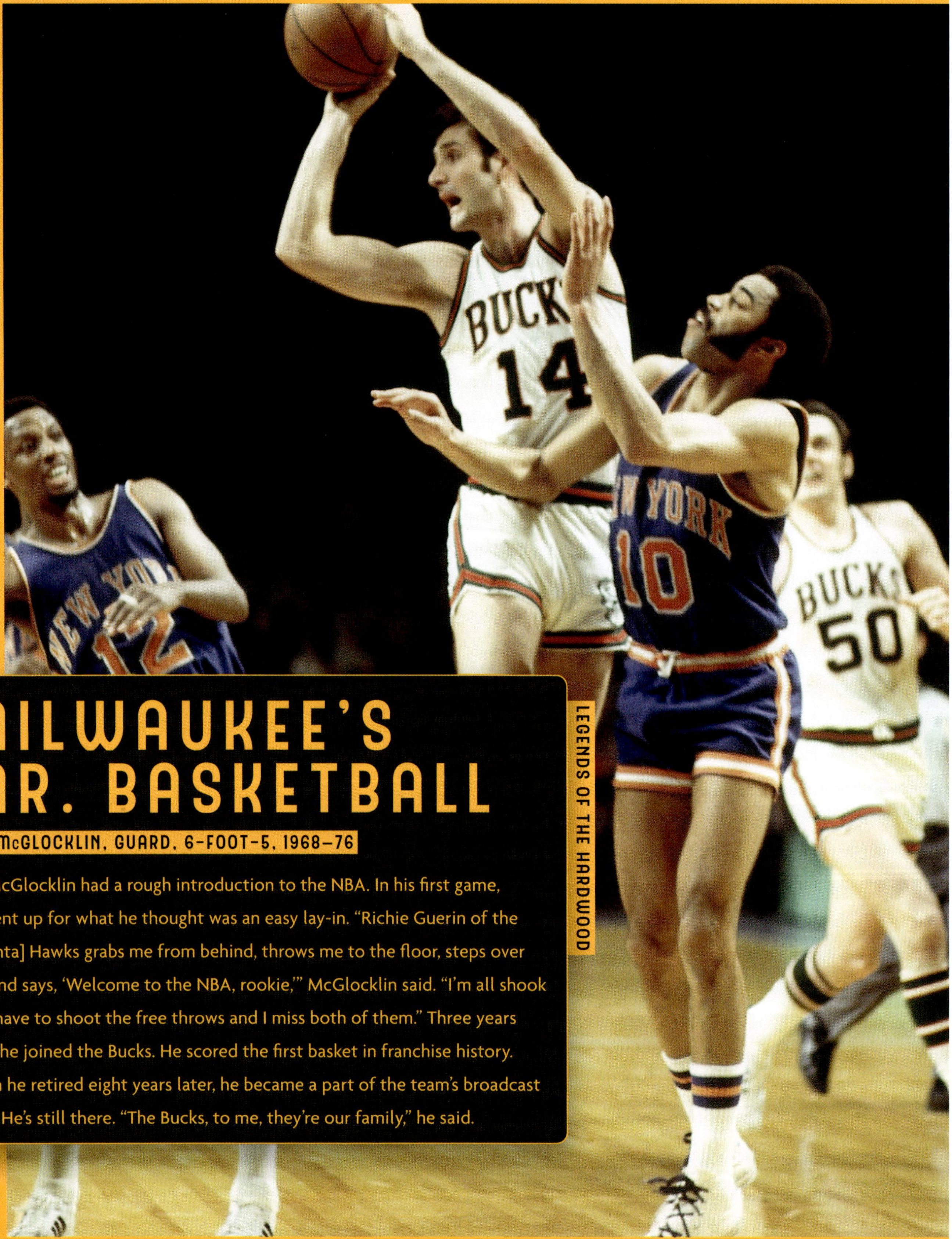

LEGENDS OF THE HARDWOOD

MILWAUKEE'S MR. BASKETBALL

JON McGLOCKLIN, GUARD, 6-FOOT-5, 1968–76

Jon McGlocklin had a rough introduction to the NBA. In his first game, he went up for what he thought was an easy lay-in. "Richie Guerin of the [Atlanta] Hawks grabs me from behind, throws me to the floor, steps over me, and says, 'Welcome to the NBA, rookie,'" McGlocklin said. "I'm all shook up. I have to shoot the free throws and I miss both of them." Three years later, he joined the Bucks. He scored the first basket in franchise history. When he retired eight years later, he became a part of the team's broadcast crew. He's still there. "The Bucks, to me, they're our family," he said.

suggested names. They included Hornets, Ponies, Skunks, Stags, and Stallions. The most popular suggestion was Robins, after Wisconsin's state bird. The runner-up was Bucks. This referred to the male white-tailed deer common in Wisconsin woods. Team owners chose Bucks. One man who had suggested the name said, "Bucks are spirited, good jumpers, fast, and agile." Those are certainly good qualities for basketball players.

The Bucks needed all those qualities in their first season. The roster was a collection of raw rookies and players other teams didn't want. They had never played together. However, the Bucks had an especially strong backcourt. Shooting guard Jon McGlocklin averaged nearly 20 points a game. He was selected for the All-Star Game. Veteran point guard Guy Rodgers provided stability. He consistently added 10 points and 7 assists per game. The Bucks finished the season with 27 wins and 55 losses. That is the third-best first-year

In just their second season, the Bucks faced the Knicks in the division finals.

record among all NBA expansion teams. But it was the worst record in the NBA's Eastern Division that year. The Phoenix Suns had the worst record in the Western Division. Before the 1969 NBA Draft, the league conducted a coin toss between the two teams. The winner would have the first overall pick. Both teams wanted the same player. Seven-foot-two UCLA center Lew Alcindor had dominated college basketball. Now he was turning pro.

The coin toss took place in the league offices in New York City. Team representatives listened in by telephone. Phoenix had the choice. It called heads. The coin came up tails. Bucks owner Wes Pavalon was so excited that he accidentally jammed his lighted cigarette into general manager John Erickson's ear as he hugged him. "It stung a little, but I didn't notice it," Erickson said. "I didn't care, once we had Lew."

TAKING THE TITLE

But the Bucks didn't have Lew. At least not immediately. The rival American Basketball Association (ABA) also wanted Alcindor. The New York Nets of the ABA tried to sign him. Alcindor had grown

The towering **LEW ALCINDOR** (33) was named league MVP three times in Milwaukee.

With 66 wins and the championship, **MILWAUKEE** dominated the NBA in 1970–71.

up in New York City. He could play close to home if he signed with the Nets. That didn't seem to matter much to him. "The NBA made me a better offer," he said. "It was a pretty easy choice to make, given the fact that the NBA was the more established league. The ABA was maybe, maybe not."

Alcindor was an immediate sensation. He was unlike anyone who had ever played the game. "He may be the first of the 7-foot backcourt men," said teammate Fred Crawford. "He can dribble and make moves that no big man ever made before." He averaged nearly 29 points, 15 rebounds, and 4 assists a game. He was an obvious choice for Rookie of the Year. He was nearly voted the league's Most Valuable Player (MVP), too. The

LEGENDS OF THE HARDWOOD

THE TOWER FROM POWER

LEW ALCINDOR (KAREEM ABDUL-JABBAR), CENTER, 7-FOOT-2, 1969–75

Lew Alcindor led his Power Memorial high school team to 71 straight wins. He was nicknamed the "Tower from Power." In his first varsity game at UCLA, he scored 56 points. That was a school record. His signature shot was the "sky hook." He would leap upward as he raised the ball high over his head and hook it toward the hoop. He also thrilled crowds with dunks. The NCAA felt he was too dominating. It banned dunking after his first season. The ban became known as the "Lew Alcindor Rule." It lasted 10 years. UCLA won the NCAA title all three years he played. He was twice voted college Player of the Year.

Versatile guard **OSCAR "BIG O" ROBERTSON** could play any role on the court.

Bucks more than doubled their win total, to 56. They beat the 76ers in the first round of the playoffs. But the eventual NBA champion New York Knicks knocked the Bucks out in the second round.

Milwaukee made two major additions the following year. One was guard Lucius Allen. He had been Alcindor's college teammate. The other was guard Oscar Robertson. He had played 10 years for Cincinnati. "The 'Big O' is the player against whom all others labeled 'all-around' are judged, and he may remain the standard forever," claims the NBA's website. The Bucks surged to 66 wins, by far the league's best record that year. Alcindor won the MVP award. The Bucks swept the Baltimore Bullets to win the NBA championship. "We won the world championship in the Bucks' third year of existence," Alcindor said years later. "That's something that I'll be proud of all of my life."

Before the 1971–72 season, Alcindor changed his name to Kareem Abdul-Jabbar. His new name reflected his Islamic faith. The Bucks continued to play at a high level for the next three years. Twice more, Abdul-Jabbar was named MVP. But Milwaukee couldn't win another NBA title. It came close in 1974. The Bucks played the Boston Celtics in the Finals. But Allen was injured before the series began. Boston won, 4–3. Robertson retired before the next season. Allen left in a midseason trade. Milwaukee struggled to a 38–44 mark. It was the first time the Bucks hadn't made the playoffs since Abdul-Jabbar's arrival. When the Bucks drafted him, he had said, "I was disappointed that I couldn't go play where I wanted to play—either in New York or San Francisco or Los Angeles." Now he felt it was time to go where he really wanted to play. He asked team officials to trade him to the Los Angeles Lakers. They did.

LEGENDS OF THE HARDWOOD

THE ONE WHO GOT AWAY

ALEX ENGLISH, SMALL FORWARD, 6-FOOT-7, 1976–78

Milwaukee chose Alex English in the 1976 Draft. The Bucks were trying to rebuild after Kareem Abdul-Jabbar left. But English never cracked the starting lineup. He averaged only 10 minutes a game. Things picked up a little in his second season. Both his playing time and scoring nearly doubled. But English was frustrated with his limited role. He signed with the Indiana Pacers. He averaged about 16 points a game with Indiana. He became a star when he was traded to Denver. No one scored more points in the 1980s. English was the first player to score at least 2,000 points in 8 straight seasons. He was an eight-time All-Star.

DOWN, UP, DOWN AGAIN

Milwaukee struggled for the next four seasons. It had just one winning record. Things changed in 1979–80. Once again, a dominating big man was the key. Milwaukee obtained

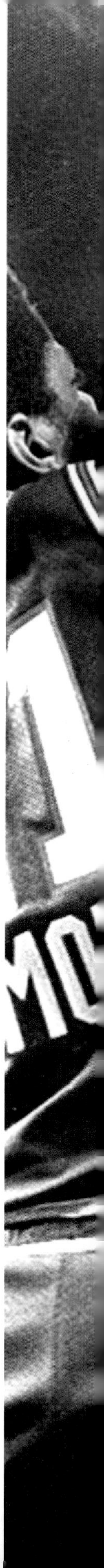

Bruising center **BOB LANIER** boosted the Bucks to the top of the division five times.

Nicknamed "Sid the Squid," **SIDNEY MONCRIEF** was a team player and a fan favorite.

> "IT'S A SHAME WE NEVER WON A CHAMPIONSHIP WITH THOSE TEAMS," MONCRIEF SAID. "WE ALWAYS HAD CHAMPIONSHIP HEART."

massive 6-foot-11 center Bob Lanier in a midseason trade with the Detroit Pistons. He joined rookie guard Sidney Moncrief, the team's top draft choice. They helped the team return to the winning column with 49 victories. The Bucks won a whopping 60 games in 1980–81 and followed up with 55 wins in the next season. But they fell in the first round of the playoffs in all three of those seasons.

In 1982–83, and again in 1983–84, Moncrief was named Defensive Player of the Year. "That guy is amazing," said Celtics star forward Larry Bird. "It's obvious he takes pride in doing whatever it takes to win." Moncrief helped the Bucks advance to the Eastern Conference finals both years. They lost 1–4 to the 76ers the first time. The second time, it was Boston that knocked off the Bucks. Lanier retired. The Bucks responded by winning 59 games in 1984–85. They won 57 and 50 the next two seasons. Each time, they won the first round of the playoffs. But returning to the championship game proved elusive.

A disappointed Moncrief finally left Milwaukee after the 1988–89 season. "It's a shame we never won a championship with those teams," he said. "We always had championship heart." The team's victory totals fell off slightly the next two years. Milwaukee still made the playoffs. But the pattern of early elimination continued.

The wheels started coming off in the 1991–92 season. The team went 31–51. It was the first time the Bucks had missed the playoffs in 12 years.

The top draft pick in 1994, forward **GLENN ROBINSON** spent eight seasons in Milwaukee.

The team had losing records for the next six seasons. The low point came in 1993–94. The Bucks won only 20 games. That was seven games worse than their first season's total. Rookie power forward Vin Baker was a pleasant surprise. He quickly moved into the starting lineup. He averaged more than 13 points and 7 rebounds a game. Milwaukee drafted well again the following year. It took National College Player of the Year Glenn "Big Dog" Robinson. "We know what he can do for us, for this team, for this city," Baker said. "We will all be delighted to see him." Team officials and fans were especially delighted when Robinson led all rookies in scoring. He averaged nearly 22 points a game.

LEGENDS OF THE HARDWOOD

NEVER SAY DIE

MILWAUKEE BUCKS AT ATLANTA HAWKS, NOVEMBER 25, 1977

The Bucks weren't having a good night. With 8 minutes and 43 seconds left, they trailed the Hawks by 29 points. The score was 111–82. Making things even more difficult, they were playing on the road. Remarkably, from that point on, the Bucks scored 35 points. Their stifling defense limited Atlanta to just four points. Forward Marques Johnson sank two free throws in the final second. Milwaukee won, 117–115. It is the greatest fourth-quarter comeback in NBA history. Only four teams have come back from deficits of 30 or more points. None except Milwaukee did it entirely in the fourth quarter.

Energetic **VIN BAKER** led the Bucks in scoring and rebounding in 1995–96.

KARL SHOWS THE WAY

Robinson and Baker helped Milwaukee improve to 34 wins in 1994–95. But the Bucks fell back to 25–57 the following season. Immediately after the 1996 Draft, the Bucks traded

Forward **TIM THOMAS** showed promise early on, but he never became an All-Star.

for slick-shooting rookie Ray Allen. His three-pointers were especially deadly. "You think you're doing pretty well against this kid, and then you look up, and he's got 20 points," said Minnesota Timberwolves guard Doug West. Despite all these additions, though, the Bucks posted losing records in the next two seasons.

Milwaukee made another important move after the 1997–98 season. The team hired George Karl as coach. He had coached in Seattle for seven years. His teams won at least 55 games almost every season. "This team has talent," Karl said when he was hired, "but they need to play together and learn defensive discipline." His first season at the helm was shortened because of labor issues. Yet the Bucks went 28–22. Despite playing 32 fewer games, the team's win total was just 6 under the previous year's. The Bucks returned to the playoffs.

BUCKS

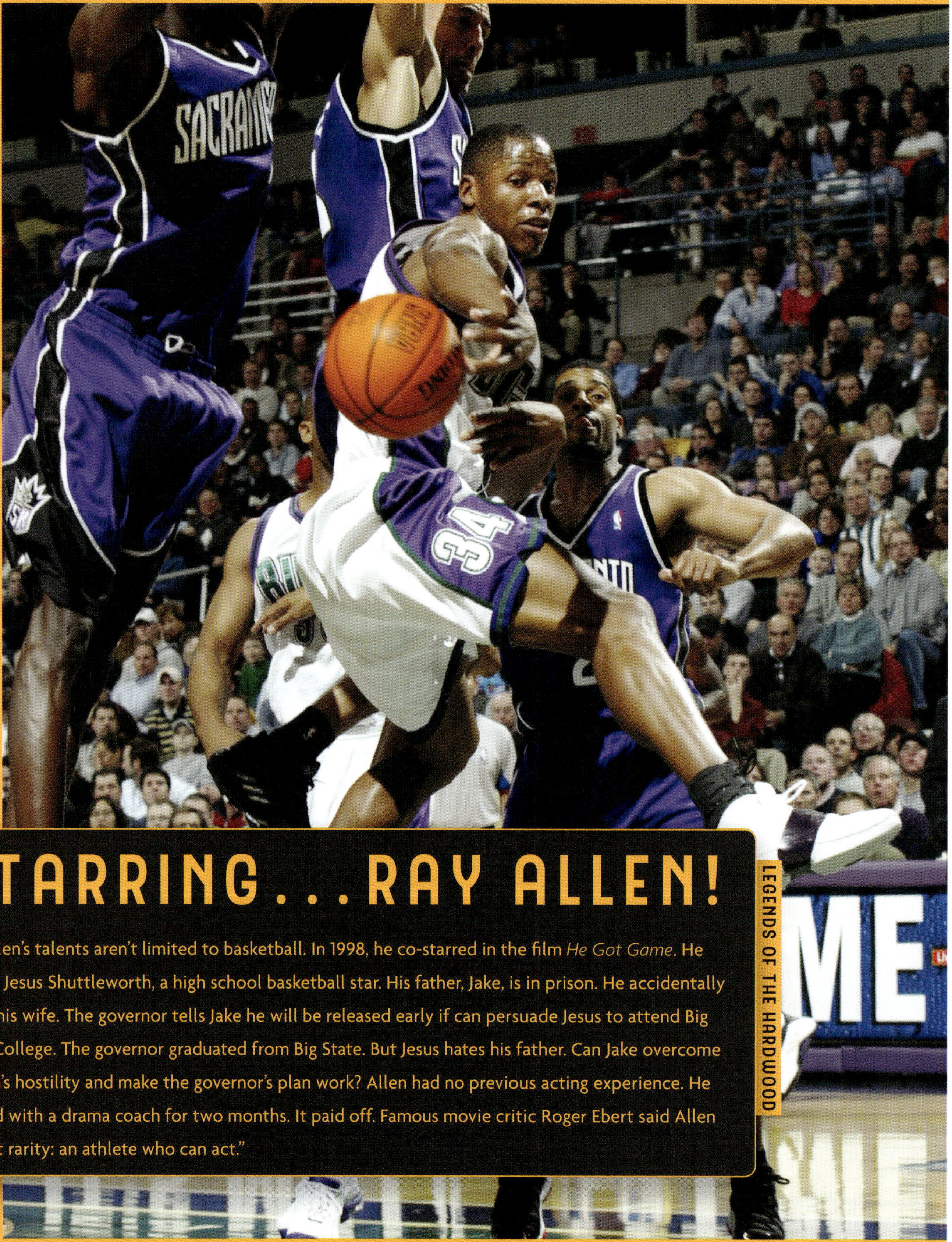

STARRING...RAY ALLEN!

LEGENDS OF THE HARDWOOD

Ray Allen's talents aren't limited to basketball. In 1998, he co-starred in the film *He Got Game*. He played Jesus Shuttleworth, a high school basketball star. His father, Jake, is in prison. He accidentally killed his wife. The governor tells Jake he will be released early if can persuade Jesus to attend Big State College. The governor graduated from Big State. But Jesus hates his father. Can Jake overcome his son's hostility and make the governor's plan work? Allen had no previous acting experience. He trained with a drama coach for two months. It paid off. Famous movie critic Roger Ebert said Allen "is that rarity: an athlete who can act."

The Pacers swept them in the first round. After that, Milwaukee added point guard Sam Cassell for veteran leadership. Along with Robinson and Allen, Cassell formed Milwaukee's "Big Three." The Bucks faced the Pacers again in the 2000 playoffs. The series came down to Allen's final desperation shot. It missed. The Pacers won, 96–95. "We played them tough," Robinson said. "But a loss like this makes us realize we can do great things."

It seemed like Milwaukee would do great things in 2000–01. The Bucks won 52 games. It was their highest win total in 15 years. Even better, they won the first two rounds of the playoffs. They faced the 76ers in the conference finals. They led the series, 2–1. Philadelphia won Game 4 to even the series. The Bucks lost Game 5 in heartbreaking fashion.

SAM CASSELL was a solid shooter and a savvy leader on the floor.

"IT NEVER SHOULD HAVE COME DOWN TO THAT," ROBINSON SAID. "WE BASICALLY GAVE THEM 10 POINTS. WE HAVE TO MAKE SURE THAT IF WE GO DOWN WE GO DOWN PLAYING THE RIGHT WAY."

Robinson missed a short jumper in the final seconds, and Allen couldn't tip in the rebound. "It never should have come down to that," Robinson said. "We basically gave them 10 points. We have to make sure that if we go down we go down playing the right way." They did play the "right way" in the following game. The Bucks tied the series. Allen tied the NBA record for three-point shots in a playoff game. But he was injured in the deciding Game 7. Philadelphia's Allen Iverson torched the Bucks for 44 points. The Sixers won easily, 108–91.

The near miss gave Bucks fans high hopes for 2001–02. Unfortunately, injuries to key players led to a 41–41 mark. Milwaukee missed the playoffs by a single game. It improved by a single game the following season. But the team lost in the first round of the playoffs. Karl, Allen, Cassell, and Robinson were all gone by 2003–04. The Bucks split the season, 41–41.

IN THE HUNT

Milwaukee fell to 30–52 the following season. Though two other teams had more losses, the Bucks had the top choice in the 2005 NBA Draft. They chose Australian-born 7-foot center Andrew Bogut. "The people of Milwaukee, no matter what, they do everything very, very hard," Bogut

ANDREW BOGUT notched 16 points, 10 rebounds, and 2.5 blocks per game in 2009–10.

LEGENDS OF THE HARDWOOD

SQUAD 6

ANDREW BOGUT, CENTER, 7 FEET, 2005–12

Andrew Bogut wanted to add noise and excitement to home games. “A lot of times it was very, very quiet,” he said. So in 2009, Bogut bought 100 seats for every game. To fill those seats, he held auditions. He wanted to see who was loudest and rowdiest. The winners formed Squad 6. Six was Bogut’s jersey number. It also stood for the “sixth man,” supporting the five players on the court. “It’s only 100 people,” Bogut said, “but the noise they make sounds like 1,000. It gives us some energy to feed off.” Some opponents also liked Squad 6. “Those fans were the most fun fans I have seen on the road *ever*,” said Dallas Mavericks owner Mark Cuban. “It made the atmosphere 100 times better.”

In his two Bucks seasons, **BRANDON KNIGHT** led the team in scoring and assists.

said. "That's exactly like I am. When I do something, I go full steam. I respect a city that prides itself on hard work." Bogut's hard work earned him a spot on the All-Rookie First Team. The Bucks improved by 10 wins to a 40–42 mark. They also qualified for the playoffs. Detroit sent the Bucks home, taking the first round 4–1. The Bucks dropped back to the bottom of the division the following three seasons. From there, the playoffs remained well out of reach.

That situation changed in 2009–10. The Bucks leaped to a 46–36

Sharpshooting guard **MICHAEL REDD** once hit eight three-pointers in a quarter.

record. They would have done even better. Bogut was having his best season yet. But he suffered a late-season injury. He was still named to the All-NBA Third Team. It was the first time an Australian had received All-Pro honors. Milwaukee took a 3–2 series lead over the Atlanta Hawks in the first round of the playoffs. But it couldn't hold on.

The Hawks won the next two games to take the series. "We did the best we could," said ultra-quick rookie point guard Brandon Jennings. "We showed a lot of people that the Milwaukee Bucks can actually hang in this league."

In just his 7th NBA game,
BRANDON JENNINGS
netted 55 points altogether.

A key player on offense and defense, **KHRIS MIDDLETON** was sidelined for much of 2016–17.

Once again, though, the Bucks couldn't maintain that momentum. Fans suffered through another four straight losing seasons, capped by a miserable franchise-worst 15–67 mark in 2013–14. Despite the losses, a core of talented young players, such as second-year shooting guard Khris Middleton and rookie small forward Giannis Antetokounmpo, gained valuable experience. The Bucks added 2014 Rookie of the Year point guard Michael Carter-Williams in a midseason trade. Carter-Williams helped the team finish the 2014–15 season at 41–41. The Bucks squeezed into the playoffs. But they lost to the Chicago Bulls in the first round. That marked the sixth playoff appearance in a row that the Bucks had suffered first-round elimination. Milwaukee took a step backwards the following season. The team's 33–49 record was far from playoff contention. In 2016–17, the Bucks improved to 42–40. Perhaps the main reason was the continued development of Antetokounmpo. The "Greek Freak" led the Bucks to a dominant win over Toronto in Game 1 of the first round of the playoffs, raising hopes for Milwaukee's first series win since 2000–01. But the Raptors came back to win four of the next five. The dream would have to wait.

The Bucks got off to one of the best starts in NBA history by winning the championship in just their third year of existence. They haven't won another title since then, though they came close on a couple of occasions. Fans hope that the team's young talent will result in another championship banner in the near future.

SELECTED BIBLIOGRAPHY

Ballard, Chris. *The Art of a Beautiful Game: The Thinking Fan's Tour of the NBA*. New York: Simon & Schuster, 2010.

Hareas, John. *Ultimate Basketball: More Than 100 Years of the Sport's Evolution*. New York: DK, 2004.

Hubbard, Jan, ed. *The Official NBA Basketball Encyclopedia*. 3rd edition. New York: Doubleday, 2000.

NBA.com. "Milwaukee Bucks." http://www.nba.com/bucks/.

Simmons, Bill. *The Book of Basketball: The NBA According to the Sports Guy*. New York: Ballantine, 2009.

Sports Illustrated. *Sports Illustrated Basketball's Greatest*. New York: Sports Illustrated, 2014.

WEBSITES

DUCKSTERS BASKETBALL: NBA
http://www.ducksters.com/sports/national_basketball_association.php

Learn more about NBA history, rules, positions, strategy, drills, and other topics.

JR. NBA
http://jr.nba.com/

This kids site has games, videos, game results, team and player information, statistics, and more.

Note: Every effort has been made to ensure that any websites listed above were active at the time of publication. However, because of the nature of the Internet, it is impossible to guarantee that these sites will remain active indefinitely or that their contents will not be altered.

INDEX